YOU'LL NEVER WALK ALONE

LIVERPOOL
FOOTBALL CLUB

EST·1892

Designed by Duncan Cook

A Grange Publication

ISBN 978-1-910199-59-6

Contents

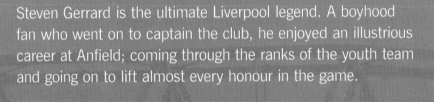

Steven Gerrard is the ultimate Liverpool legend. A boyhood fan who went on to captain the club, he enjoyed an illustrious career at Anfield; coming through the ranks of the youth team and going on to lift almost every honour in the game.

At his peak he was comparable with the finest midfielders in Europe and is genuinely regarded as arguably the greatest player to ever pull on the famous red shirt.

One of the most famous footballers on the planet, his fame spreads way beyond the confines of his native Merseyside, and in the year that he finally severed his long ties with his beloved Liverpool to begin an exciting new chapter of his life in Los Angeles, this annual celebrates the very best of Stevie G by reliving the many memorable moments that have helped make him so special.

STEVIE
THROUGH THE SEASONS

For 17 years Steven Gerrard was an almost constant presence in the Liverpool first team – a period in which he played under five different managers and helped the club win seven major trophies...

1998/1999

GAMES: 6
GOALS: 0
HIGHLIGHT: Making his debut v Blackburn

1999/2000

GAMES: 31
GOALS: 1
HIGHLIGHT: Scoring first senior goal v Sheffield Wednesday

2000/2001

GAMES: 50
GOALS: 10
HIGHLIGHT: Helping Liverpool win the treble

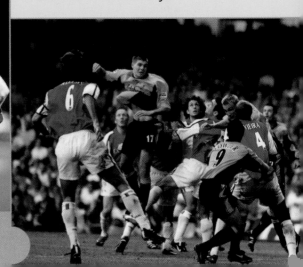

2001/2002
GAMES: 45
GOALS: 4
HIGHLIGHT: Playing in the Champions League for the first time

2002/2003
GAMES: 54
GOALS: 7
HIGHLIGHT: Netting Liverpool's first goal in the Worthington Cup final victory over Manchester United

7

2003/2004
GAMES: 47
GOALS: 6
HIGHLIGHT: Being handed the Liverpool captaincy on a permanent basis

2004/2005
GAMES: 43
GOALS: 13
HIGHLIGHT: Lifting the Champions League trophy

2005/2006
GAMES: 53
GOALS: 23
HIGHLIGHT: Scoring twice in the FA Cup final

2006/2007
GAMES: 51
GOALS: 11
HIGHLIGHT: Leading Liverpool to another Champions League final

9

2007/2008

GAMES: 52
GOALS: 21
HIGHLIGHT: Becoming Liverpool's all-time leading goalscorer in European competition

2008/2009

GAMES: 44
GOALS: 24
HIGHLIGHT: Scoring two goals in a 4-0 win over Real Madrid

2009/2010

GAMES: 49
GOALS: 12
HIGHLIGHT: Captaining England at the World Cup in South Africa

2010/2011

GAMES: 24
GOALS: 8
HIGHLIGHT: Coming off the bench to score a 2nd half hat-trick v Napoli

2011/2012
GAMES: 28
GOALS: 9
HIGHLIGHT: Lifting the
Carling Cup at Wembley

2012/2013
GAMES: 46
GOALS: 10
HIGHLIGHT: Winning his
100th England cap

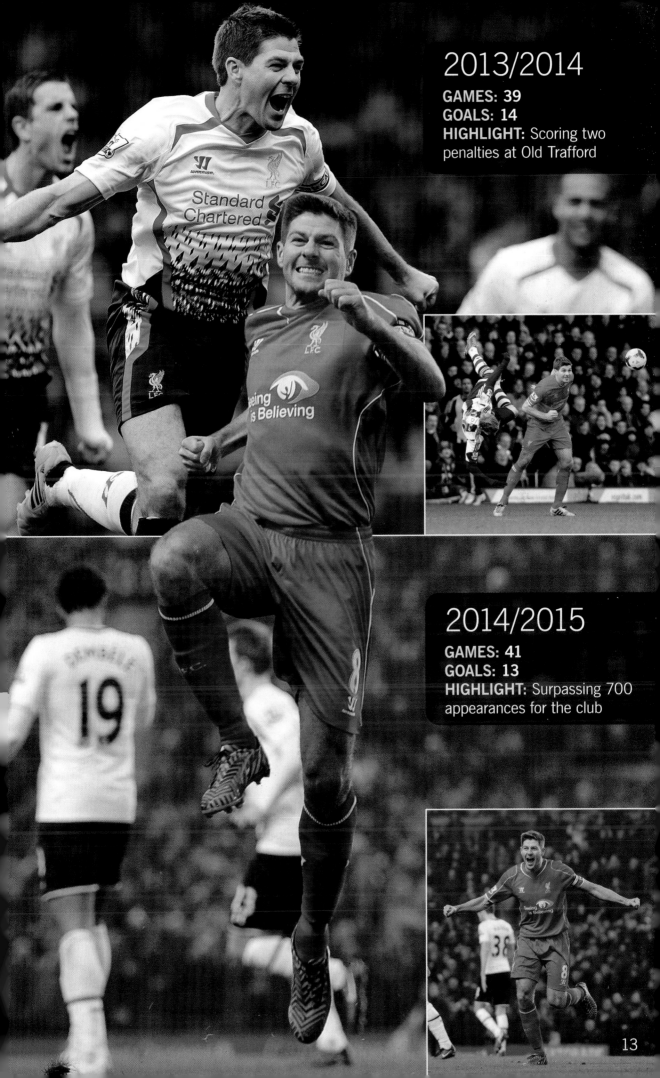

2013/2014

GAMES: 39
GOALS: 14
HIGHLIGHT: Scoring two penalties at Old Trafford

2014/2015

GAMES: 41
GOALS: 13
HIGHLIGHT: Surpassing 700 appearances for the club

SPOT THE DIFFERENCE

Can you spot 10 differences between the pictures below?

Answers on p 61.

15

STEVEN GERRARD
CAREER IN NUMBERS

4
The number of successive European games at Anfield in which he scored - a feat never achieved by a Liverpool player before.

5
His tally of hat-tricks in a Liverpool shirt, all of them at Anfield.

6
He has found the net half a dozen times as a substitute in European games for Liverpool. No player has scored more coming off the bench for the club in Europe.

7
His highest tally of goals against a goalkeeper during his career so far - Jussi Jaaskelainen (all with Bolton) and Tim Howard (all with Everton).

8
Steven's collection of winners medals includes three in the League Cup, two FA Cup and one each in the European Cup, UEFA Cup and European Super Cup.

13
The tally of goals he has scored against Aston Villa - more than against any other team.

15
The length of time in minutes it took him to score a second-half hat-trick as a substitute against Napoli in the Europa League in 2010.

16
The number of successive seasons that the Reds captain has scored in, holding the club record - one more than Billy Liddell.

19
Steven's age when he scored his first Liverpool goal - in a 4-1 win against Sheffield Wednesday in December 1999.

24
He has found the net against 24 different teams in European competitions with the most (5) coming against Total Network Solutions.

24
The highest tally of goals he has recorded in a single season for the Reds (2008-09).

28
The shirt Steven wore when he made his first-team debut as a last-minute substitute against Blackburn in 1998.

33
The number of times he has faced the Blue half of the city in derby clashes, netting on ten occasions.

41
His total of goals in Europe for the Reds - comfortably a club record and the most by any British player for an English club in Europe.

47
The penalties he has successfully converted for Liverpool in 57 attempts - a success rate of 82%.

51
He is only the second player to score 50 or more goals for the club away from home in the Premier League.

54
His most prolific season for club appearances - 2002-03. One of which was the League Cup final victory over Manchester United in which he scored.

65
The number of different teams he has scored against with Queens Park Rangers being the last one he got off the mark against.

87
His tally of appearances for the club in Europe's most prestigious club competition, the Champions League.

101
The number of different goalkeepers he has found the net against.

104
The number of times Steven has found the net at Anfield in a red shirt - 56% of his goals have been scored in front of the Kop.

104
Steven scored more goals for Liverpool under Rafa Benitez than any other player.

114
He has won more than a century of caps for England, making his debut against Ukraine at Wembley in May 2000.

115
The number of different teams he has played against from AC Milan to Zenit St Petersburg.

120
Steven's tally of goals accumulated in the Premier League.

121
His number of goals scored in the second half of games - none were scored during a period of extra-time.

124
The number of times he found the net for Liverpool during the 'Noughties' - more than any other player.

160
The number of Liverpool players he has shared a pitch with during his career; the latest being Jerome Sinclair against Chelsea in May.

186
His goal tally - currently in fifth place on the club's all-time list, behind only Ian Rush, Roger Hunt, Gordon Hodgson and Billy Liddell.

310
The average number of minutes between Steven Gerrard goals for Liverpool Football Club.

470
His tally of appearances as Liverpool captain - wearing the armband for the first time against Southampton in the League Cup in 2002.

647
The total number of games that Steven started during his Anfield career.

3,132
The number of consecutive minutes Steven played from the start of the 2012-13 Premier League campaign - a sequence that only ended when injury forced his substitution at Newcastle in April.

57,629
His total number of minutes on the pitch as a Reds player during a most illustrious career.

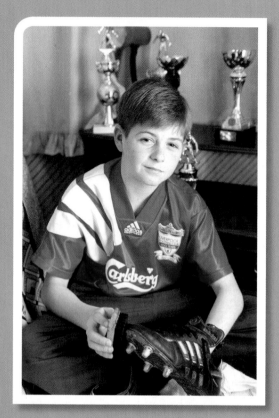

The Making of a SUPERSTAR

Steven Gerrard was born in Whiston hospital on 30 May 1980 and brought up in nearby Huyton. Home for the Gerrards was Ironside Road on the Bluebell Estate and it was here that a young Stevie first honed his skills.

At every opportunity he would be out the in street playing football with his mates but one day it nearly cost him his future career. While trying to retrieve a ball that had gone into the nettles on a piece of wasteland, Gerrard attempted to kick it clear but succeeded only in getting the prongs of a hidden garden fork lodged in his big toe.

As he lay writhing around in pain an ambulance was called and Gerrard was quickly whisked off to Alder Hey Children's Hospital where the doctors had to be persuaded not to amputate his toe, a procedure that could have prematurely curtailed his promising career.

By this point Gerrard's potential had been spotted by Liverpool scouts. He first came to their attention while playing for Whiston Juniors and started to attend the club's Centre of Excellence, the forerunner of the Academy.

Under the watchful eye of coaches Steve Heighway, Hugh McAuley and Dave Shannon, Gerrard's talent was carefully nurtured. His progress was overshadowed slightly by that of Michael Owen, but he soon caught up.

He made his first appearance in the 'B' team shortly before his 15th birthday and was 16 years of age when he was called up for his reserve team debut in February 1997, a 3-2 victory at home to Leeds.

In November that year Gerrard signed his first professional contract and twelve months later was pushing for a place in the first team squad, after being brought to the attention of manager Gerard Houllier.

He travelled with the squad for the away leg of Liverpool's UEFA cup tie against Celta Vigo, where he was an unused substitute, then came off the bench to make his senior bow at home to Blackburn the following weekend.

The rest is history.

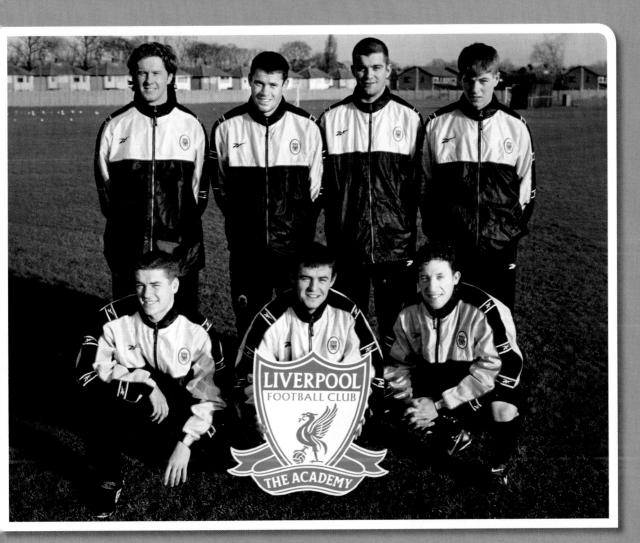

Steven Gerrard is a RED

From as far back as he can remember Steven Gerrard has been a Liverpool fan. His dad had supported the club all his life and Stevie followed suit.

He attended his first game at Anfield in November 1986. It was League Cup replay against Coventry City. He sat in the Kemlyn Road stand (now known as the Lower Centenary) and watched as Jan Molby scored a unique hat-trick of penalties in a 3-1 win for Kenny Dalglish's team.

"I'd just started at the club's Centre of Excellence," he

recalls. "I was given tickets by Steve Heighway, and just knowing that I was going to a game at Anfield for the first time was like the buzz you

get when looking forward to Christmas Day. I loved every minute of it. I remember just coming out and seeing the pitch for the first time and

it looked surreal; the grass looked greener, the lights were so bright and it just looked like the perfect stage. That's where the dreams began really."

As he got older, Gerrard started going to games with his brother Paul and stood on the old Spion Kop terrace. "I went to lots of games back then. Even when I started full-time at Liverpool at 16 years of age, I'd go to the majority of matches."

He cites John Barnes as being his first big Liverpool hero then later he looked up to the likes of Steve McManaman, Jamie Redknapp and Robbie Fowler, all of whom he later played alongside in the Reds' first team.

Find the words in the grid. Words can go horizontally, vertically and diagonally in all eight directions.

```
E D Q R X E D L E I F D I M L
U R L R T K N T Y D C P B X D
G M B E G N R G R X H Y K Y O
A Y Q H I N C A L C K G P L O
E R I P J F R N A A O N S V W
L E S Q R R N R R A N S Z Q L
S U T R E G D A L J A D M G E
N R A G J I H S L P T N G C M
O O N B F L I V E R P O O L N
I P B F H Q T N H T V R O I N
P E U K M Z N E V U Z F A H C
M L L L H L R V W R Y T F D S
A G V L M L T E V G P T M P T
H E L K C A T T F A Q M O G L
C F A C U P X S C V J K Y N M
```

STEVEN	MIDFIELD	ENGLAND
GERRARD	ANFIELD	EUROPE
LIVERPOOL	MELWOOD	GOALS
HUYTON	CAPTAIN	TACKLE
ISTANBUL	FACUP	SHOOT
CARDIFF	CHAMPIONSLEAGUE	PASS

Answers on p 61

Great Moments – Istanbul 2005

On May 25, 2005, Steven Gerrard scaled his highest peak. The Ataturk Stadium in Istanbul was the setting and late that night he lifted the greatest prize in club football.

Liverpool's journey to Champions League glory that year had been an incredible one.

It was Gerrard's stunning late goal against Olympiacos that secured qualification to the knockout phase and memorable victories over Juventus and Chelsea followed before the final showdown with AC Milan.

When the Italian giants raced into a three-goal lead Gerrard's dream was looking a forlorn one. Within nine minutes of the second half starting the Liverpool skipper gave his team a lifeline by glancing a header into the top corner of the Milan net.

Five minutes later and the Reds had remarkably drawn level, through goals by Vladimir Smicer and Xabi Alonso, the latter scoring on the rebound from a penalty awarded after Gerrard had been brought down in the box by Gennaro Gattuso.

The game went into extra-time and Gerrard continued to perform a true captain's role, filling in all over the pitch to prevent Milan regaining the lead.

With no further goals scored a penalty shoot-out was required to decide the destiny of the trophy and Gerrard was down to take Liverpool's fifth kick. Fortunately, the heroics of goalkeeper Jerzy Dudek meant he wasn't required.

When Dudek saved a penalty from Andriy Shevchenko Liverpool were confirmed as Champions of Europe for a fifth time and Gerrard followed in the illustrious footsteps of the club's previous European Cup winning captains – Emlyn Hughes, Phil Thompson and Graeme Souness – in proudly taking possession of the trophy that is known around Anfield as 'old big ears'.

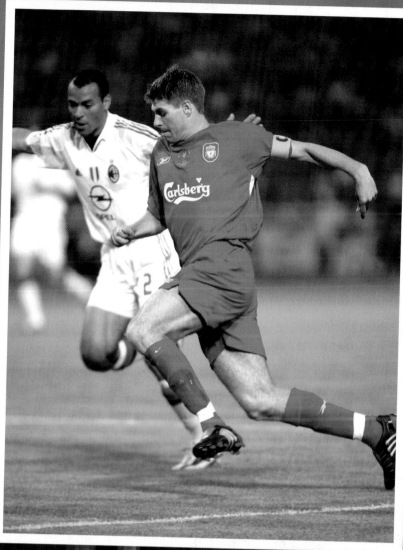

Gerrard's Top 10 Goals

Headers, volleys, long-ranger screamers, tap-ins, free-kicks and penalties – Steven Gerrard has scored them all. But what are the ten best goals he's netted in a Liverpool shirt? It's an almost impossible task to whittle them down but how about these...

10 Inter Milan (H) – 19 FEBRUARY 2008

On a typically tense European night in front of the Kop, Gerrard kept his composure to grab a vital second goal for the Reds with just a few minutes remaining. He took possession of the ball out on the right and powered a low shot into the far corner.

8 Everton (A) 15 SEPTEMBER 2001

Brutal and direct, Gerrard lashed the ball back across the face of the goal, where it spun beyond Paul Gerrard and into the top corner of the net, sparking a famous celebration that saw him run the length of the Bullens Road stand with the tongue out.

9 Marseille (A) – 16 SEPTEMBER 2008

A breathtaking goal that demonstrated everything: poise, agility, vision, power and much more. The Reds countered down the field, Kuyt found Gerrard, who dug the ball out from beneath his feet and sent it spiraling

7 Southampton (H) 1 JANUARY 2001

A young Stevie picked the ball up just inside the opposition half, surged forward and unleashed a pearler, which rocketed 45 yards, bounced down off the underside of the bar and into the Kop net.

6 Aston Villa (A) 11 AUGUST 2007

A sumptuous free-kick that got Liverpool's season off to a winning start. Gerrard won the set-piece by drawing a foul on the edge of the Villa box and stepped up to curl the ball into the top corner for a last-gasp 2-1 win.

3 Olympiakos (H) 8 DECEMBER 2004

Liverpool led 2-1 but one more goal was required to secure qualification to the knockout phase of the Champions League. When Mellor's header bounced into the path of Gerrard, the skipper expertly manoeuvred his body in order to arrow the ball low into the back of the net.

5 Manchester United (H) 31 MARCH 2001

Robbie Fowler's cushioned pass near the halfway line found its way to Gerrard, who unleashed a sensational strike that left Fabian Barthez rooted to the spot. It was his first ever goal against United and it won the BBC Goal of the Month award.

2 West Ham United (MILLENNIUM STADIUM) 13 MAY 2006

With minutes left on the clock, players cramping up on the pitch and West Ham fans jigging with delight in the stands, he swiped at a loose ball 30 yards from goal and sent it crashing into Shaka Hislop's net to take the game to extra-time.

4 Middlesbrough (H) 30 APRIL 2005

1 AC Milan (ATATURK STADIUM) 25 MAY 2005

One of the most brilliant long-range efforts Anfield has ever witnessed. The moment the ball bounced up at chest height in front of Stevie, the ground was on its feet in expectation. Gerrard's stunning, dipping half-volley didn't disappoint.

So many special memories were borne out of this sensational leap and powerful twist of the neck. Not only was it a truly vital goal, but it was a superbly executed one too.

Stevie G's LFC Dream Team

He's been tipped by many to one day embark on a career in management but if he had to pick a 'dream team' of players that he played alongside for Liverpool during his time at the club this is the XI Steven Gerrard would send out onto the pitch...

Pepe Reina

Nationality: Spanish
Position: Goalkeeper
Years at LFC: 2005-2013
Games: 394
Goals: 0

Jamie Carragher

Nationality: English
Position: Centre back
Years at LFC: 1996-2013
Games: 737
Goals: 5

Sami Hyypia

Nationality: Finnish
Position: Centre back
Years at LFC: 1999-2009
Games: 464
Goals: 35

Markus Babbel

Nationality: German
Position: Right back
Years at LFC: 2000-2004
Games: 73
Goals: 6

Glen Johnson

Nationality: English
Position: Left back
Years at LFC: 2009-2015
Games: 200
Goals: 9

Dietmar Hamann

Nationality: German
Position: Midfield
Years at LFC: 1999-2006
Games: 283
Goals: 11

Himself

Nationality: English
Position: Midfield
Years at LFC: 1998-2015
Games: 710
Goals: 186

Xabi Alonso

Nationality: Spanish
Position: Midfield
Years at LFC: 2004-2009
Games: 210
Goals: 19

Luis Suarez

Position: Striker
Nationality: Uruguayan
Years at LFC: 2011-2014
Games: 133
Goals: 82

Robbie Fowler

Nationality: English
Position: Striker
Years at LFC: 1993-2001
& 2006-07
Games: 369
Goals: 183

Fernando Torres

Nationality: Spanish
Position: Striker
Years at LFC: 2007-2011
Games: 142
Goals: 81

STEVIE'S SHIRT SWAPS

Throughout the course of his career Steven Gerrard has accumulated a vast collection of memorabilia, the majority of which is now currently on display at the Liverpool FC Museum.

As well as the many medals that he's won, there's also a huge amount of shirts that he's swapped with opposition players after matches, ten of which we feature here...

Paolo Maldini (AC Milan)

Trofeo Santiago Bernabéu
Santiago Bernabéu Stadium
4 August 2002

Dennis Bergkamp (Arsenal)

FA Premier League
Highbury
12 March 2006

Pep Guardiola (Barcelona)

UEFA Cup semi-final 2nd leg
Anfield
19 April 2001

Andrea Pirlo (Italy)

World Cup Group D
Arena de Amazonia
14 June 2014

Alan Shearer
(Newcastle United)

FA Cup 4th round
Anfield
24 January 2004

Zlatan Ibrahimovic (Inter Mi

Champions League round of
1st leg
Anfield
19 February 2008

Xavi Hernandez (Barcelona)

Champions League round of 16 1st leg
Nou Camp
21 February 2007

Alessandro Del Piero (Juventus)

Champions League quarter-final 1st leg
Anfield
5 April 2005

Teddy Sheringham (West Ham United)

FA Cup final
Millennium Stadium, Cardiff
13 May 2006

Andriy Shevchenko (AC Milan)

Champions League final
Ataturk Stadium, Istanbul
25 May 2005

In His Own Words

The key moments of Steven Gerrard's career, as described by the man himself...

Signing his first professional contract

"The sums were mind-boggling, but it was never, ever about money. It was just about the football. Going full-time as a professional is one of the greatest feelings I have had in football."

His Liverpool debut versus Blackburn in November 1998

"I remember being anxious to impress in those first few minutes, so I just tried to keep things simple. I made a few passes that were short and safe, but also over-hit a couple of crosses. I was running on adrenaline and trying too hard to make an impact."

Making his senior England debut at Wembley

"I'd watched many, many cup final and international games at Wembley and only ever dreamed of running out to play a football match. It was such a high, a dream come true."

Scoring in England's famous 5-1 rout of Germany

"It was certainly one of the highlights of my career to score against Germany. My touch was perfect for once and I got fantastic contact – the pitch was wet and I put enough power on it to slide past a top keeper."

Being named Liverpool captain

"That was one of the best days of my life. Growing up, it was certainly something that I always strived for. I was captain of my school side and I used to go along to Anfield to watch the team and I always looked up to people like John Barnes who captained the team during the 90s. I used to watch Barnes with the captain's armband and dream that one day it would be me captaining the team I love."

2005 Champions League final

"I don't think there are enough words to describe what happened that night. It's difficult to explain fully. I've tried my best on so many occasions, but there's still so much more to add. In the 18 years I've been a professional; it's certainly the most special game that I've ever played in."

Deciding not to join Chelsea in 2005

"I love Liverpool so much. This is my club. My heart is with Liverpool. I don't need to tell anyone that. Everyone who knows me can see how I feel. The last thing I wanted to do was leave, I just couldn't do it."

Scoring an injury-time equaliser against West Ham in the 2006 FA Cup final

"Just before my second goal I had taken a free-kick and it nearly went out of the stadium, my legs were so weary, so I don't quite know where I got the energy from. I must admit I was absolutely delighted to hit the next shot like that. I didn't mean to put it exactly there but knew I had to get good contact to make sure it would hit the target and I caught it really sweetly. It was a great moment when it went in, and I don't know how I did it. I just concentrated on giving everything to the shot."

Lifting the League Cup on Liverpool's first appearance at the new Wembley in 2012

"Again, we did it the tough way; another penalty shoot-out. I actually missed a penalty, but I lifted the cup, so it doesn't matter. It was great for me personally and great because it meant we'd won another cup. Some people disrespect the League Cup and try to knock it, but when you're representing Liverpool in a major cup final, especially under the managership of Kenny Dalglish, it means everything."

On almost winning the Premier League in 2013/14

"It's such a huge low for me and for everyone at the Club. We got so close and the journey we were on was unbelievably enjoyable. I genuinely thought it was our turn. I thought this was going to be it, the one I haven't got. But we gave it everything we could. But it didn't happen. We just fell short at the end. It's heartbreaking and it will be for a long, long time."

Playing at Anfield for the final time before moving to LA Galaxy

"It felt very strange. I've been dreading this moment and the reason being is because I'm going to miss it so much. I've loved every minute of it and I'm absolutely devastated I'm never going to play in front of these supporters again."

SPOT THE BALL

Can you spot the location of the ball?

Answers on p 61.

ALL THE TROPHIES

Steven Gerrard is one of the most decorated Liverpool players of recent times. These are the games in which he claimed his winners' medals...

League Cup
25 FEBRUARY 2001

Millennium Stadium, Cardiff
Liverpool 1 v 1 Birmingham City*

FA Cup
12 MAY 2001

Millennium Stadium, Cardiff
Liverpool 2 v 1 Arsenal

UEFA Cup 16 MAY 2001

Westfalenstadion, Dortmund
Liverpool 5 v 4 Alaves

Super Cup 31 AUGUST 2001

Stade Louis II, Monaco
Liverpool 3 v 2 Bayern Munich

League Cup 2 MARCH 2003

Millennium Stadium, Cardiff
Liverpool 2 v 0 Manchester United

FA Cup 13 MAY 2006

Millennium Stadium, Cardiff
Liverpool 3 v 3 West Ham United*

Community Shield 13 AUGUST 2006

Millennium Stadium, Cardiff
Liverpool 2 v 1 Chelsea

European Cup 25 MAY 2005
Ataturk Stadium, Istanbul
Liverpool 3 v 3 AC Milan*

League Cup
26 FEBRUARY 2012

Wembley Stadium,
London
Liverpool 2 v 2
Cardiff City*

(*Liverpool won on
penalties)

THE GERRARD Quiz

How well do you know Stevie G? Tackle our bumper quiz and see how you fare?

1. What is Steven Gerrard's middle name?
A: James
B: Paul
C: George

2. Other than '8' what other two numbers has Gerrard worn for Liverpool?
A: 17 & 33
B: 28 & 33
C: 17 & 28

3. Which player did Gerrard replace when making his first team debut for Liverpool in November 1998?
A: Stig Inge Bjornebye
B: Vegard Heggem
C: Bjorn Tore Kvarme

4. In which city did Gerrard score his first England goal?
A: Munich
B: Madrid
C: Milan

5. Who were the opponents when Gerrard captained Liverpool for the first time?
A: Stoke City
B: Southampton
C: Sunderland

6. At which stadium did Gerrard collect his first winners' medal in a Liverpool shirt?
A: Wembley
B: Millennium
C: Ataturk

7. During the Champions League winning campaign of 2004/05, Gerrard scored against Olympiacos, AC Milan and which other club?
A: Grazer AK
B: Bayer Leverkusen
C: Juventus

8. Which of the following World Cups did Gerrard not appear in?
A: 2002
B: 2006
C: 2010

9. Who did Gerrard swap shirts with at the end of the 2005 Champions League final?
A: Shevchenko
B: Maldini
C: Pirlo

10. In what year did Gerrard win the PFA Player of the Year award?
A: 2001
B: 2006
C: 2009

11. Against which club did Gerrard come off the bench and score a hat-trick?
A: Napoli
B: Everton
C: Total Network Solutions

12. Which club has Gerrard scored most goals against?
A: Everton
B: Aston Villa
C: West Bromwich Albion

13. How many times did Gerrard win the League Cup?
A: Once
B: Twice
C: Three times

14. In 2012, Gerrard became the first Liverpool player to do what?
A: Represent his country at the European Championships
B: Lift a trophy at the new Wembley
C: Score a hat-trick against Everton

15. Against which country did Gerrard win his 100th England cap?
A: Sweden
B: Germany
C: France

16. Who did Gerrard succeed as Liverpool's most prolific penalty taker?
A: Ian Rush
B: Johh Barnes
C: Jan Molby

17. Which team provided the opposition for Gerrard's testimonial?
A: AC Milan
B: Olympiacos
C: Real Madrid

18. In the list of Liverpool's all-time leading goalscorers, where does Gerrard rank?
A: 5th
B: 3rd
C: 10th

19. Only two other players have made more appearances for Liverpool than Gerrard, Ian Callaghan and who?
A: Billy Liddell
B: Kenny Dalglish
C: Jamie Carragher

20. Which former Anfield team-mate will Gerrard be linking up with at LA Galaxy?
A: Robbie Keane
B: Daniel Agger
C: Djimi Traore

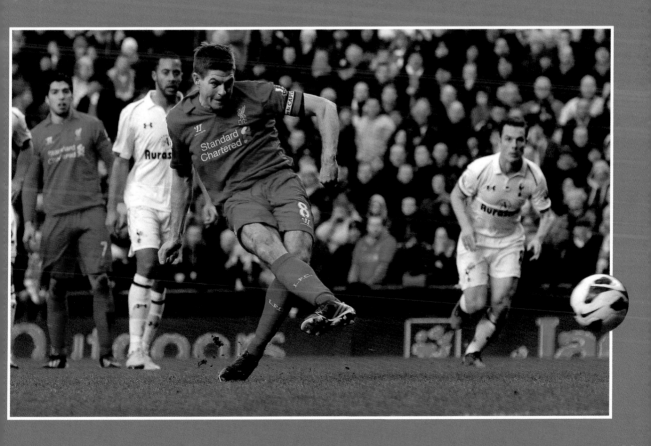

Answers on p 61.

Stinging the Blues

As a red-hot Liverpudlian Steven Gerrard enjoyed nothing better than scoring against city rivals Everton, and during the course of his 17 years in the Liverpool first team he netted ten times at the expense of the Blues. These are some of the highlights…

15 September 2001 Everton 1 v 3 Liverpool
In front of the Gwladys Street side he celebrated his first derby goal and this 11th minute strike set Liverpool on their way to a 3-1 triumph

28 December 2005 Everton 1 v 3 Liverpool
The captain helped make this a Christmas to remember for the red half of Merseyside by adding to Peter Crouch's early goal and making it 2-0 after just 18 minutes

25 January 2009 Liverpool 1 v 1 Everton
A goal nine minutes after the break cancelled out Everton's first half lead and secured a replay in this evenly fought FA Cup fourth round tie

3 March 2012 Liverpool 3 v 0 Everton
Stevie became the first player to score a hat-trick in the Merseyside derby since Ian Rush in 1982 as he single-handedly fired Liverpool to a comfortable Anfield victory

28 January 2014 Liverpool 4 v 0 Everton
With just a point separating Liverpool and Everton in the Premier League table a tight encounter was expected but when Stevie scored after 21 minutes it opened the floodgates for the Reds to go on and record their biggest derby win for three decades

Stevie G's DERBY FACT-FILE

- Gerrard scored more goals against Everton than any other team apart from Aston Villa
- The only player to score more Liverpool goals against Everton is Ian Rush
- In total he made 33 appearances in the Merseyside derby and was on the losing side just five times
- On his derby debut in April 1999 he famously cleared off the line in a 3-2 Liverpool win
- He captained Liverpool to victory over Everton in the FA Cup semi-final at Wembley in April 2012

Stevie Stats

A statistical look back on Steven Gerrard's Liverpool career...

APPEARANCES & GOALS

League	504	120
FA Cup	42	15
League Cup	30	9
Europe	130	41
World Club Championship	2	1
Community Shield	2	0
TOTAL	**710**	**186**

MILESTONE APPEARANCES

	Date	Against	Stadium	Competition
1	29.11.1998	Blackburn Rovers	Anfield	League
50	23.09.2000	Sunderland	Anfield	League
100	11.09.2001	Boavista	Anfield	Europe
150	28.09.2002	Manchester City	Maine Road	League
200	28.09.2003	Charlton Athletic	The Valley	League
250	23.11.2004	Monaco	Stade Louis II	Europe
300	05.11.2005	Aston Villa	Villa Park	League
350	22.10.2006	Manchester United	Old Trafford	League
400	28.10.2007	Arsenal	Anfield	League
450	18.10.2008	Wigan Athletic	Anfield	League
500	05.12.2009	Blackburn Rovers	Ewood Park	League
550	05.01.2011	Blackburn Rovers	Ewood Park	League
600	04.11.2012	Newcastle United	Anfield	League
650	12.01.2014	Stoke City	Britannia St.	League
700	04.02.2015	Bolton Wanderers	Reebok Stadium	FA Cup
710	24.05.2015	Stoke City	Britannia St.	League

WHEN STEVEN'S GOALS HAVE COME

	Goals	%
0-15 minutes	15	8.06
16-30 minutes	20	10.75
31-45 minutes	30	16.13
46-60 minutes	39	20.97
61-75 minutes	42	22.58
76-90 minutes	40	21.50
Total	**186**	

FIRST HALF/SECOND HALF GOALS

	Goals	%
FIRST HALF	65	34.95
SECOND HALF	121	65.05

MILESTONE GOALS

	Minute	Date	Against	Stadium	Competition
1	69	05.12.1999	Sheffield Wednesday	Anfield	League
50	40	25.10.2005	Crystal Palace	Selhurst Park	League Cup
100	76	01.10.2008	PSV Eindhoven	Anfield	Europe
150	41	09.08.2012	Gomel	Anfield	Europe
186	70	24.05.2015	Stoke City	Britannia St.	League

GROUNDS HE HAS SCORED AT MOST

Anfield	104
Upton Park	6
Old Trafford	5
St James' Park	5
Villa Park	5
Reebok Stadium	4
Britannia Stadium	4
Stade Velodrome	3
Millennium Stadium	3
White Hart Lane	3

GOALKEEPERS HE HAS SCORED MOST GOALS PAST

Tim Howard (Everton)	7
Jussi Jaaskelainen (Bolton)	7
Gerard Doherty (Total Network Solutions)	5
Shay Given (Newcastle)	5
Joe Hart (Birmingham & Man City)	5
David James (Aston Villa, West Ham, Man City & Portsmouth)	5
Heurelho Gomes (PSV Eindhoven & Tottenham)	4
Robert Green (West Ham & QPR}	4
Brad Guzan (Aston Villa)	4
Steve Mandanda (Marseille)	4

STEVEN GERRARD AS CAPTAIN
(games when he has started as captain only)

	PLD	W	D	L	PTS	WIN %
Premier League	343	174	89	80	611	50.73
FA Cup	28	17	3	8	-	60.71
League Cup	17	10	2	5	-	58.82
Champions League	59	32	12	15	-	54.24
UEFA Cup/Europa League	21	13	3	5	-	61.90
World Club Championship	2	1	0	1	-	50.00
Total	**470**	**247**	**109**	**114**	**-**	**52.55**

A Liverbird among Three Lions

It's not just with a Liverbird on his chest that Steven Gerrard has excelled as a footballer.

He's been equally proud to wear the Three Lions of his country and is one of just nine players to have won over 100 England caps. Here are some interesting stats and facts about Gerrard's international career...

- In total, he made 114 England appearances and scored 21 goals

- He first represented his country at under-16 level, making five appearances

- He also played for the under-18s (2 appearances) and under-21s (4 appearances, 1 goal)

- He made his senior debut on 31 May 2000, a 2-0 win against Ukraine at Wembley

- His first appearance at a major tournament was in June 2000 when he came

off the bench in England's European Championship group game against Germany

- The first goal he scored for England also came against Germany, during

an emphatic 5-1 win in Munich in September 2001

- Three of his international caps were won at Anfield, where England played Finland (2001), Paraguay (2002) and Uruguay (2006)

- During the first 21 games he played for England, Gerrard was never once on the losing side

- In 2007 and 2012 he was voted England player of the year

- On 31 March 2004 he captained his country for

the first time, away to Sweden, and went on to wear the armband 38 times

- He has played under 8 different England managers – Kevin Keegan, Howard Wilkinson, Peter Taylor, Sven-Goran Eriksson, Steve McLaren, Fabio Capello, Stuart Pearce and Roy Hodgson

- Gerrard made his landmark 100th England appearance in Sweden on 14 November 2012

- In becoming an England centurion he followed in the footsteps of Billy Wright, Bobby Charlton, Bobby Moore, Peter Shilton and David Beckham. Frank Lampard, Ashley Cole and Wayne Rooney have also since joined this exclusive club

- He is one of just 13 England players to have represented his country in three World Cup finals. He featured at Germany 2006, South Africa 2010 and Brazil 2014

- His last international appearance came at the 2014 World Cup, a goalless draw against Costa Rica in Belo Horizonte, Brazil

- No Liverpool player has won more international caps than him

Tributes

Steve Gerrard's contribution to the Liverpool cause will never be forgotten, here's a selection of tributes from some of the biggest names who managed him, played alongside him and played against him...

"The first time I saw him I knew he'd be Liverpool captain one day. It was always going to be there for him. Some players carry themselves differently, the way they portray themselves around the training ground - you could see the way he was watching, wanting to learn."

JAMIE REDKNAPP, LFC PLAYER 1991-2002

"Steven's love for LFC was something that really shone through. We saw him develop from an enthusiastic boy into a world-class player."

STEVE HEIGHWAY, LFC ACADEMY DIRECTOR 1989-2007

"Stevie is a very inspirational leader. Somebody who inspires, somebody who leads, somebody you want to follow. He pulls the team through in difficult times. That is why I made him captain."

GERARD HOULLIER, LFC MANAGER 1998-2004

"I'd put him in the top three, not just in England but in the world because he's a complete player, someone who's always made the difference ever since he was young. Would I have liked to play alongside him? I think anyone would love to play with players of that calibre."

FRANCESCO TOTTI, AS ROMA PLAYER 1992-PRESENT

"I'm sure he's going to be remembered forever as one of the biggest - if not the biggest - legends in the club. And that's huge; it's Liverpool - one of the biggest clubs in the world. I'm sure he's very proud of that and I'm very proud of him. I would have liked for Stevie to play for Liverpool forever and forever."

FERNANDO TORRES, LFC PLAYER 2007-11

"He is one of the best players in the world. He's got an aura around him; he's got that

ning not everyone has. Not everyone has
 fear factor but he's got a fear factor and
e's still got it to this day because of all he's
chieved and what he still does now as well.
've got nothing but love and respect for the
uy, for everything he's achieved."
DANIEL STURRIDGE, LFC PLAYER 2013-PRESENT

He was so inspirational. When Stevie was
on your side you knew that he could produce
moments of magic. I remember the goal
gainst Olympiacos or the FA Cup final goal
gainst West Ham, both came out of nothing.
For me, he's been one of the players that I
most enjoyed playing alongside."
XABI ALONSO, LFC PLAYER 2004-09

He is one of the best players in the world. I
had watched him on TV and it was a dream
o play with him at Liverpool. It was a
pleasure to be on the pitch with Stevie."
LUIS SUAREZ, LFC PLAYER 2011-14

I think the most important thing is the
people who have seen him play have been
very privileged to have watched him. We
were absolutely blessed to watch somebody
who has lived for the football club, has
saved the football club on many an occasion
with his performances on the pitch, and
someone who did it humbly and did it
fantastically well."
KENNY DALGLISH, LFC MANAGER 2011-12

He will always be a legend for Liverpool.
He has won the Champions League and he
has won the FA Cup. He is an icon for the
club, a legend and someone that everybody
will remember."
RAFAEL BENITEZ, LFC MANAGER 2004-2010

"I think Steven has been and is an
absolutely complete player, because he had
personality, technique, he could set the
play and also defend, and he could score
goals - penalty-kicks, free-kicks. So really
a modern and complete player. His story is
one of those stories to be told, one of those
fairytales - to be narrated to your children
and grandchildren"
PAOLO MALDINI, AC MILAN PLAYER 1985-2009

He's a player that I really thought a lot of;
I had a lot of time for him and rated him.
I can't say that about everyone. Why did
I like him so much? Perhaps there was
something about him that reminded me a
little bit of myself."
ZINEDINE ZIDANE, JUVENTUS PLAYER 1996-2001
& REAL MADRID PLAYER 2001-2006

"I always think Steven's a player who has
moments in games that no-one else can
touch, the moments which take your breath
away. And that's what makes him different to
virtually every other player of his time."
JAMIE CARRAGHER, LFC PLAYER 1996-2013

Great Moments – Cardiff 2006

Just under 12 months after the miracle of Istanbul, Steven Gerrard's divine intervention guided Liverpool to more silverware.

This time, victory was achieved much closer to home. The prize at stake was the FA Cup and Cardiff's Millennium Stadium was the stage on which we witnessed arguably, one of the greatest individual performances of all-time.

Again, a thrilling fight-back was required. With only half an hour gone against West Ham, Liverpool found themselves two goals down and chasing the game. A searching through ball by Gerrard set up Djibril Cisse to quickly reduce the arrears and early

in the second half, the captain took centre stage by drawing the Reds level with an unstoppable half-volley from 12-yards out.

Liverpool were then expected to go on and win the game but Paul Konchesky went up the other end ten minutes later and shocked everyone by restoring the Hammers' advantage.

There seemed to be no way back for the Reds now and when the stadium clock signaled that the 90 minutes

Anfield for a seventh time.

Not since the great Stanley Matthews way back in 1953 had one player dominated a FA Cup final in this way and because of that it will now forever be remembered as the 'Gerrard final'.

were up it looked all over, the claret and blue ribbons were being tied to the cup in preparation.

Then, a minute into injury time the ball fell to Gerrard 30-yards from goal and the number 8 unleashed a thunderous shot that whistled beyond the despairing dive of Shaka Hislop. Liverpool had been saved by their skipper once again.

To cap a truly herculean display Gerrard then went and converted a penalty in the shoot-out and the FA Cup was on its way back to

ICTURE QUIZ

's one of the most photographed footballers in the world but take a look at ese four snaps and see if you can remember some of the vital details.

Name the year?

Name the opponent?

Name the stadium?

Name the occasion?

Answers on p 61.

Did You KNOW?

Brush up on your knowledge with a selection of must-know Stevie G facts and figures...

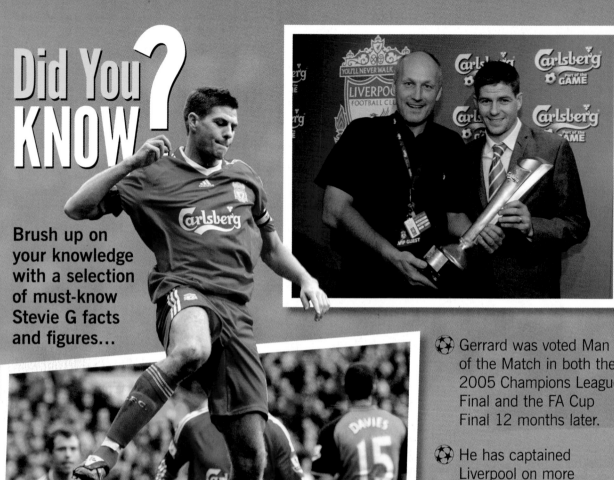

⚽ Gerrard was voted Man of the Match in both the 2005 Champions League Final and the FA Cup Final 12 months later.

⚽ He has captained Liverpool on more occasions than any other player – 470 times – and is the club's longest-serving captain – more than 11 years.

⚽ Gerrard became the second youngest captain to lift the European Cup when the Reds won the trophy in 2005.

⚽ When scoring in the 2006 FA Cup final, he became the first man ever to score in the finals of the FA Cup, League Cup, UEFA Cup and Champions League; he remains the only man to have done so.

⚽ Gerrard lies third in the club's all-time appearances list with 710. The player immediately above him is Jamie Carragher, who played 737 games. Out in front is Ian Callaghan with 857.

⚽ He won more international caps while with Liverpool than any other British-born Reds player – 114 for England.

⚽ No player has scored more penalties in a Liverpool shirt than Gerrard. He has successfully converted 47 times, five more than Jan Molby who previously held the record.

⚽ Gerrard has scored five hat-tricks for the club – against Aston Villa and Everton in the league, Luton Town in the FA Cup, Total Network Solutions in the Champions League and Napoli in the Europa League.

⚽ The club he scored most often against in a Liverpool shirt is Aston Villa – 13 of his goals have come against the Midlanders.

- Gerrard is the last Liverpool player to be voted PFA Young Player of the Year, winning the award in 2001.

- He started his Liverpool career wearing the number 28 shirt before switching to number 17 and eventually to number 8 in 2004 following the sale of Emile Heskey.

- As a schoolboy Gerrard once had a trial with Manchester United.

- He has been named in the PFA Premier League Team of the Year on eight occasions – 2001, each year from 2004 to 2009 and 2014.

- His most prolific season for Liverpool was in 2008/09 when he scored 24 times.

- Gerrard was awarded an MBE in the 2007 Queen's New Year Honours List and made

an Honorary Freeman of his home borough of Knowsley in 2008.

- He captained Liverpool for the first time in a 3–1 League Cup victory over Southampton at Anfield, a season before he was

given the armband on a permanent basis.

- His 186 goals have been scored against 101 different goalkeepers including six who at one time have played for the Reds: David James, Brad Friedel, Paul Jones, Brad Jones, Chris Kirkland and Simon Mignolet.

- He is fifth on the list of Liverpool's all-time leading goalscorers. Only Billy Liddell, Gordon Hodgson, Roger Hunt and Ian Rush have bettered his tally of 186

- Gerrard scored 41 goals for Liverpool in Europe, the most by any British player in the history of European competition.

- 104 of those goals have been scored in front of his home crowd.

CROSSWORD

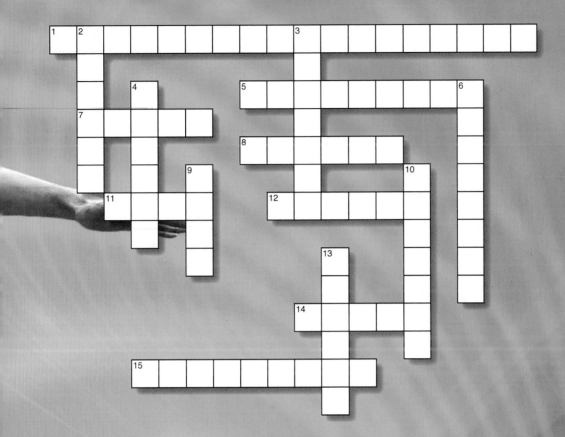

ACROSS

1 Against which club did Steven Gerrard score his first Liverpool goal?

5 Name the Everton goalkeeper who Steven Gerrard scored three goals past in March 2012?

7 How many children does Steven Gerrard have?

8 LA ------, the name of Steven Gerrard's new club?

11 How many hat-tricks did Steven Gerrard score for Liverpool?

12 Who did Steven Gerrard succeed as Liverpool captain in 2003?

14 What country staged the 2005 Club World Championship final?

15 Who scored an own goal for Liverpool in the 2006 FA Cup final?

DOWN

2 In what area of Merseyside did Steven Gerrard grow up?

3 At what ground did Steven Gerrard win his first full England cap?

4 In which country did Steven Gerrard make his last England appearance?

6 Who was Liverpool manager when Steven Gerrard lifted the Carling Cup in 2012?

9 With what part of his body did Steven Gerrard score in the 2005 Champions League final?

10 Who was AC Milan's captain for the 2005 and 2007 Champions League finals?

13 Name Liverpool's opponents in the 2001 UEFA Cup final?

In A Galaxy Far Far Away...

As Steven Gerrard embarks on a new adventure in America here's all you need to know about his new club LA Galaxy and the league they play in.

⚽ Other notable players to have played for Galaxy include David Beckham and Landon Donovan

⚽ Galaxy were founding members of the MLS in 1996 and are its most decorated club

⚽ They have a mascot called Cozmo and cheerleader group called the Galaxy Star Squad

⚽ The StubHub Center is the second-largest purpose built soccer stadium in the MLS

Founded: 1995

Home Ground: StubHub Center, Carson, California

Capacity: 27,000

Colours: White, Navy Blue & Gold

Nickname: Los Galacticos

Main rivals: San Jose Earthquakes

Head Coach: Bruce Arena

Captain: Robbie Keane

Honours: MLS Cup 2002, 2005, 2011, 2012, 2014

CONCACAF Champions Cup 2000

Lamar Hunt US Open Cup 2001, 2005

MLS Supporters' Shield 1998, 2002, 2010, 2011

Major League Soccer

The MLS consists of 20 clubs, split into two divisions – the Western and Eastern Conference. Each team plays 34 games, 24 against those in their conference and 10 from the other. The regular season runs from March to October, with a 12-team play-off

Competing teams in the 2015 MLS Western Conference	Competing teams in the 2015 MLS Eastern Conference
Colorado Rapids	Chicago Fire
FC Dallas	Columbus Crew SC
Houston Dynamo	DC United
LA GALAXY	Montreal Impact
Portland Timbers	New England Revolution
Real Salt Lake	New York City FC
San Jose Earthquakes	New York Red Bulls
Seattle Sounders FC	Orlando City SC
Sporting Kansas City	Philadelphia Union
Vancouver Whitecaps	Toronto FC

...aking place in November, ...ollowed by the MLS Cup ...inal in early December. ...he Supporters' Shield is ...warded to the team that ...acks up the most points ...uring the season. Five ...eams from the MLS also ...ompete in the CONCACAF ...hampions League.

Quiz/Puzzle Answers

WORDSEARCH p20

SPOT THE DIFFERENCE p21

SPOT THE BALL p34

THE GERRARD QUIZ p38

1. C	6. B	11. A	16. C
2. C	7. A	12. B	17. B
3. B	8. A	13. C	18. A
4. A	9. A	14. B	19. C
5. B	10. B	15. A	20. A

PICTURE QUIZ p53

Name the year?	2002
Name the stadium?	Old Trafford
Name the opponent?	Paul Gascoigne
Name the occasion?	All star charity match at Anfield in March 2015

CROSSWORD p57

Where's Stevie?